Lemon Pie

Lessons From Unlikely Places To
Nourish You In Troubled Times

Amelia Jo Mitchell, Psy.D.

WestBow
PRESS
A DIVISION OF THOMAS NELSON

WestBow Press books may be ordered through booksellers or by contacting:

WestBow Press
A Division of Thomas Nelson
1663 Liberty Drive
Bloomington, IN 47403
www.westbowpress.com
1-(866) 928-1240

ISBN: 978-1-4497-7465-3 (e)
ISBN: 978-1-4497-7466-0 (sc)
ISBN: 978-1-4497-7467-7 (hc)

Library of Congress Control Number: 2012920972

Printed in the United States of America

WestBow Press rev. date:11/16/2012

Contents

Dedicated to

My children and all children to follow with love and wisdom from past generations.

"All religions teach that we should love one another; that we should seek out our own shortcomings before we presume to condemn the faults of others, that we must not consider ourselves superior to our neighbors."

Anonymous.
Statement to the forty-fourth session of the United Nations Commission on Human Rights
February 17, 1988
Geneva

Preface

In a country blessed with incredible wealth, resources, and opportunities, forty million Americans over the age of eighteen seek treatment for anxiety disorders, and one in ten (or 18.8 million) are diagnosed with a depressive disorder according to the 2011 figures from the CDC (Center for Disease Control). That is 18 percent and 9.5 percent of the United States population, respectively, and these figures do not account for those individuals who are not seen by a treatment provider. $48 billion of our national healthcare budget is spent on treating anxiety disorders alone.[1] What can account for such an unprecedented prevalence of mood disorders?

Our society offers excuses for the bad (sometimes illegal) behavior of our leaders and role models and focuses on the immediate gratification of the self, possessions, and technology over human connection. This book was written in the hope that it may offer an accessible remedy for some of our ills and a reminder that there are better ways to live that may help ameliorate much of our distress. I believe that each of us is accountable for the contribution we make to this world and that by taking responsibility for ourselves, we will provide succor to our own souls for, in my way of thinking, the immeasurable cost is to the human spirit.

The idea of this book was first conceived while searching for a wedding present for my oldest son and his bride that would be a unique gift of love from Mother. Through my own life experience and many hours of counseling others, I knew that the love they felt so strongly at the beginning of their life journey together would be tested by the daily vicissitudes of life. Love and marriage, after all, are dynamic and are influenced by both internal and external forces.

But I am more than a mother. I am also a clinical psychologist and have spent much of my adult life listening to people in acute pain. I have walked briefly with them on their paths from heartache to health and hopefully helped them realize that they have power to change their lives if they accept responsibility and learn to live with generous, kind spirits.

The lessons that I have been taught by family, friends, and even strangers and recorded in this book are pertinent to all of us. They are about integrity, kindness, and taking responsibility for oneself, for that is the best any of us can strive for. Through the years, I have learned to recognize patterns that we humans seem to share in various degrees, despite our uniqueness. I share thoughts about relationships with you, sometimes offering advice as I do when counseling others, and sometimes reflecting back on my own life experience.

I offer what I know to be true, what I believe to be true, and random thoughts about how I learned about love and life. Take from it what you might find useful. My hope is that you will identify with at least one of these little vignettes and mindfully review your own life story. Perhaps this book can be a ready resource for encouragement when the quotidian tasks of life weigh you down and you forget that love, both of oneself and for others, really must remain the focus if life is to be joyous and satisfying.

Some parts of this missive speak more to the individual, some more to couples, and others to interactions in the broader community. I believe that the lessons contained herein are apropos to any relationship and worth consideration. It is through relationships with others that we learn who we are and how we fit into society. How we treat others has more impact than we might imagine; this fact is no more evident than in these stories I relate. I am quite certain that my sixth-grade classmate of whom I write in "Compassion" would be surprised that his kindness left a lifelong impression on me, as would my friend who helped heal a very hurt part of my heart as I relate in "Our Own Worst Critic."

I believe that we all have love stories. These stories begin when we take our first breaths—when life is full of potential and promise. There is no doubt that each of us will face challenges, insecurities, fear, and heartbreak as the years unfold. But life also presents laughter and joy, overwhelming beauty, and the opportunity to experience great pride as we use the talents and gifts bestowed upon us. What we choose to focus on and nourish will, in many ways, determine not only who we become, but also the tenor of the world we live in and leave to our children.

You Have a Love Story

Perhaps you have just proclaimed your love in front of family and friends and are beginning your life as a couple. You are crazy in love with one another and thrill to the joy of actually beginning your life together.

Countless others have been where you find yourselves right now, but that is not the beginning of your love story. Many believe they need the other in order to be complete; you do not. In my way of looking at things, people marry for many reasons. Often, these reasons have more to do with what is perceived as "getting" rather than "giving." And that is, quite frankly, wrong thinking and too often unsustainable.

This is not your love story.

Perhaps you have just become parents and marvel at the new life you have created. Finally, you are complete. In your arms is someone with whom you can share unconditional love. That hole of loneliness in your heart is mended.

This is not your love story, either.

A love story is truly about what we have been blessed with and give to another, not what we hope to receive in return. If our love is based on expectations, we will often be disappointed.

If you don't believe it true, think about a small child presenting a self-drawn picture to Mom with pure joy and excitement. It is given as an exquisite work of art—and it truly is, because it is the best the child has to offer. The intent is to please; in return, a smile and a few words of praise are all it takes to light the child's heart. Think of how you, as an adult, feel when you plan a surprise or choose a special gift for your beloved. In the right spirit, you are totally focused on pleasing the other—not about oneself at all. In essence, it is saying to the other, "I love you so much that I will put great time and thought into trying to find the perfect gift to let you know how much you mean to me." And it doesn't get much better than seeing genuine delight in return—affirmation that your efforts were right on target.

Your love story is already present in you; it is your birthright. It is what you have to offer another, be it a spouse, parent, child, or stranger. If we *all* recognize this and really *know* it to be true, it will continually be reciprocated … well, how can it possibly go wrong?

Life is too short or too long for me to allow
myself the luxury of living it badly.

—Paulo Coelho

Live Every Moment

I would like to share an experience I had in Okinawa, Japan. I remember it two years later with vivid clarity and hope I can describe it well enough that you hear the message.

I was sitting on a bench at the back of a wide sidewalk, waiting for the doors to open for an event I was about to attend. Many people were waiting, milling around between me and a thoroughfare—not quite a street, but certainly open to vehicular traffic. I was just watching, not up to making small talk with those around me.

I saw a very old woman wending her way down the thoroughfare. I noticed an infliction that I find particularly cruel—a type of arthritis that renders its victims horribly bent. This woman could not stand upright as she was bent from the waist at a ninety-degree angle; all she could readily see was the ground beneath her. She pulled a little cart, most likely because she had no other way of holding anything. As I watched her, I assumed that she was out doing her weekly (daily?) shopping.

I continued to watch her, feeling some pity at the cruelty that life can bestow. I assumed that because of her posture, she couldn't possibly be aware that I was observing her. As she moved

5

more into my line of sight, something quite incredible happened. When she was directly opposite me, through the legs of other bystanders, she turned her head and looked directly into my eyes. She broke into a glorious smile. In that wrinkled, old face, I saw nothing but radiant beauty. She almost seemed to say, *Don't pity me. I've had my moment, and it sustains me even now. Life is good.* She then turned back to the task at hand, moving slowly toward her destination.

I was awestruck by what had occurred between us! I couldn't explain it other than to think I had been blessed.

What I would like to share from this encounter is the fact that none of us knows what we may be called upon to endure in our lifetime. Difficulties arise for all of us in one way or another—but then we have a choice. We can struggle with the "Why me?" point of view and what we consider to be the unfairness of life. We can make ourselves unhappy with what we have lost in beauty or physical ability, what we have not gotten that we dreamed we would have, or all the ways life has been difficult. A California friend who is battling lung cancer recently wrote this:

> "We can't replace what we once had, nor have what we wished for but did not receive. We can adapt and move forward. Change is ever present, and the present and future belong to people who are willing to be in it and *live* now, creating what they can while they still have the chance. As well as moving toward what you want, be open to receiving what you have. Being open to what you have is sometimes not as easy as it sounds. It can require a disciplined awareness to be open to receive what is right in front of you. There are

usually important things waiting to be received right at our door, but we just forget to be open to them because we are busy mourning or looking for something else that we do not have."

Like the beautiful old woman in Okinawa, we can live joyously despite it all. How many people give up and decide it is too hard, embarrassing, or time-consuming to hook up their little carts and head for the streets to get on with the business of life?

Marie Howe[2] wrote the poem "What the Living Do" in memory of her brother, Johnny, who died of AIDS. She says, "For me, this poem is a reminder to see the beauty in the everyday moments—the basic comings and goings of errands and necessities, chores and minor catastrophes—because these minutes and hours add up to the days of one's life. There are so many things in this world to want, but sometimes just being alive is enough."

What the Living Do

Johnny, the kitchen sink has been clogged for days, some utensil probably fell down there.
And the Drano won't work but smells dangerous, and the crusty dishes have piled up

waiting for the plumber I still haven't called. This is the everyday we spoke of.
It's winter again: the sky's a deep, headstrong blue, and the sunlight pours through

the open living-room windows, because the heat's on too high in here, and I can't turn it off.

Amelia Jo Mitchell, Psy.D.

For weeks now, driving or dropping a bag of groceries in the
street, the bag breaking,

I've been thinking: This is what the living do. And yesterday,
hurrying along those
wobbly bricks in the Cambridge sidewalk, spilling my coffee
down my wrist and sleeve,

I thought it again, and again later, when buying a hairbrush:
This is it. Parking. Slamming the car door shut in the cold.
What you called *that yearning*.

What you finally gave up. We want spring to come and the
winter to pass.
We want whoever to call or not call, a letter, a kiss—we want
more and more and then more of it.

But there are moments, walking, when I catch a glimpse of
myself in the window glass,
say, the window of the corner video store, and I'm gripped by a
cherishing so deep

for my own blowing hair, chapped face, and unbuttoned coat
that I'm speechless:
I am living. I remember you.

It's hard to remember this as we trudge through the quotidian
tasks of life. But try hard to live life to the fullest, count your
blessings, and be content.

Be Present

Jon Kabat-Zinn[3] wrote a book called *Where Ever You Go, There You Are*. He is not the originator of the "being present in the moment" philosophy; it is the foundation of much of the Buddhist teachings. Logically, this philosophy makes sense and has merit; I've even tried to practice it. I think it is easier said than done—more so now than at any previous time.

Our capitalistic society—which runs on consumerism—has hooked us on instant gratification and wants us to believe that if we partake of every opportunity a world of technological wizardry can offer, we will be happier. We are continually available via our cell phones, have answers to almost all our questions by way of the Internet (and don't even need to access through a computer anymore), and are bombarded with too many choices because we have the whole world to browse through—no matter the cost to our pocketbooks or sanity. We don't even have to go to the store; it's all available at our fingertips. The very tools that were touted as time-savers have robbed us of down time. And if we resist, we are regarded as out of touch.

Let me remind you of life before we had the world at our fingertips; I believe this slower pace still has a valuable place in our lives. There is something to be said for disconnecting and not being on-call all the time. A more positive philosophy would encourage us to stay in the moment with those who are present with us or perhaps simply have the time to be quiet by ourselves.

I recall the beginning of all of this connection when call waiting was the newest way Ma Bell enticed us to be always available. We could have a telephone conversation with one person and be notified via a beep that someone else was calling and expected our attention. We had to make the decision to continue the first call or end it prematurely to talk to someone a bit more interesting. Perhaps call waiting was a good way to end a boring conversation, but I always thought it was the epitome of rudeness.

One of the complaints I hear frequently when counseling couples goes something like this: "The minute she walks in the door, she's on the phone with her mother" or "As soon as he finishes dinner, he gets on the computer, and I might not see him again for hours." The offenders may defend themselves by saying they are "at home" or "with her," but in actuality, they aren't available in any sense except the physical. They are certainly not in the present and are not present with their partners.

Set your priorities. There is a time for friends and family; indeed, they are integral parts of a healthy life. But make sure you reserve time for yourself that is sacrosanct; you make the decision to invite another to join you if you'd like. Turn off the electronics. Unless it's an emergency (and there really aren't that many in a person's life), understand that we aren't nearly as indispensable as we lead ourselves to believe. It's okay to let others find their own solution to boredom or deal with their moments of angst without us.

I think we need uninterrupted time to be alone, think, and enjoy being rather than always being on call. We need time to discover, be awed, relax, and appreciate the world around us without interruption from others—even friends.

Be Accountable for One

I am aware that lessons that are important for me to learn become crystallized in mantras that pop into my head at appropriate times. One of them is from my Chicago years when I was in graduate school.

A good friend and companion, Gary*, had lived in Chicago all his life, living in the same house for more than fifty years. The only child of elderly parents, he grew up on the street level of a two-flat. His parents, aunt, and uncle purchased the building together when they were newly married couples and raised their children there, so my friend grew up with three "siblings" upstairs.

When his parents died, Gary inherited half of the flat. Unfortunately, two of his three cousins (the ones he liked) had long since moved on, and the one who inherited the upper flat was Stan.* Even though he was legally blind, Stan was very bright and had a good job. He had never married and lived rather reclusively, refusing to participate in the care of the building or the yard—both the day-to-day upkeep and financially when repairs were required.

Stan became something of a hoarder; although I never saw his living space, the shared basement was filled with row after row of newspapers stacked floor to ceiling with narrow pathways left open to allow access to the laundry area. He used Gary's washer and dryer and never thought twice about asking to borrow anything he needed or wanted. He usually made these requests through curt notes left on the shared foyer table, where he would also leave the check for his portion of shared utilities.

I never knew him to do anything that Gary asked of him, like caring for Gary's dog for a night (which entailed only making sure he had food and water and letting him out into the fenced yard) or signing for a package when he was home and Gary was not. The answer was always no and usually delivered with a "how dare you ask me" attitude. I occasionally saw Stan waiting for a bus (since he couldn't drive). The first couple of times, I stopped and asked if I could give him a lift home since I was going there myself. He usually just waved me away so I stopped asking.

This cousin's attitude was especially evident and annoying when his siblings or other family members came into town and expected to stay at their old family home during their visit. Immediately, Stan would call and tell Gary that company was coming and incidentally ask, "It's okay for them to stay in your spare bedroom, right?" Even if it wasn't particularly convenient, Gary always said, "Sure."

About the third time this happened and because it interrupted plans my friend and I had already made, I finally asked in exasperation, "Why do you always say yes? He never does anything for you. He doesn't even take responsibility for his half of the house. I think you're nuts!"

Gary turned to me and calmly replied, "Because I won't let his behavior determine who I am."

Well, that took the wind right out of my sails and left me with a life lesson that I have thought of numerous times over the years. We can respond to anger with anger, injustice with injustice, insult with insult. Or we can understand that we are only responsible for and accountable to ourselves.

I will not let another's behavior determine who I am.

*Names have been changed.

The Devil Made
Me Do It

In the 1970s, a comedian became famous for his popular character, Geraldine, and her boyfriend, "Killer." Whenever she confessed to committing some undesirable behavior, she would defend her actions by stating, "The Devil made me do it," which soon became a national catchphrase.

Although it's been years since I've heard someone say, "The Devil made me do it," I frequently hear the same kind of defense when someone relates a behavior of which he or she is not proud: "*She* made me mad." "*He* got me drunk." I can't help but ask, "How did he/she do that?"

The reality is that we have no power over anyone to *make* him or her do anything he or she does not want to do. If you need evidence, try feeding a baby who doesn't want to eat what you're offering. You *might* get the food in his mouth, but chances are very good that more of the food will end up on you, the floor, or depending upon the vigorousness of rejection, even the walls than in the baby's tummy. If you can't *make* a baby eat even though your intentions are good and you have a great deal of power over him, how do you imagine that one adult can *make* another adult do anything?

We don't get angry, drunk, or anything else unless we choose to do so, so we might as well give up the blame game and place the responsibility where it belongs. We get angry because something in our environment threatens our perceived well-being, and we choose to retaliate. We continue to ignore the signs that we've had enough to drink, because the rewards of continuing to party with our friends outweigh the consequences of inebriation, at least for the moment.

Certainly, we can be influenced by others; I am in the profession of trying to influence in a positive direction. One of the most difficult lessons in graduate school was summed up by one mentor: "You can't want change for someone more than he or she wants it for himself or herself." I finally had to accept that I can't fix anyone, no matter how good my intentions or hopes for improvement of distressful symptoms. I pass that on to my clients during our initial visit: "I have no magic wand. If you choose change, you will have to do the mindful work of making it happen. I can guide you by reflecting back what I hear you say and perhaps offering another point of view. I do not have the answers to your dilemmas."

Isn't this grand? Each of us has to be responsible for just one. Speaking for myself, that's quite enough. I cannot imagine the burden of making decisions and choices for another; I don't live another person's life or suffer the consequences of what he or she does. To know you are not—and cannot be—responsible for another's happiness or well-being should come as a great relief.

Perhaps you're thinking, *You don't understand. I was raised in an abusive household. My father (mother) was an alcoholic and beat me. I had to fend for myself (and maybe siblings) to make sure I (we) had food or got to school.* You were robbed of your childhood, and I am deeply sorry for that. But still, I say to you, "You are no longer a child. Don't allow the person who took your childhood rob you of a satisfying life now that you are an adult." Don't blame your caregivers or circumstances from the past, because none of us can change the past. Your experiences may give you insight into your reactions as an adult, but move on. Make different choices now.

With responsibility comes power—a deep knowledge that you can make a difference and make good things happen in your life. Embrace it.

Lessons from an Armadillo

I just had a solitary encounter with an armadillo. I was sitting quietly outside in the dark when a lone armadillo caught my attention. It was meandering along the road, eventually moving up toward the manicured lawn of the hotel grounds. I imagine it was looking for food. I was glad that it moved away from the road, because I recalled what happens to these nocturnal animals when danger looms and fear sets in.

Armadillos have two defense mechanisms. They can either curl up in a ball, letting their tough armor plates protect their soft underbellies, or they can jump, spreading their legs and triggering the coarse guard hairs that lie under their armor to stand straight up. The second defense makes them appear larger than they actually are and hopefully intimidates and scares away the predator. That might serve armadillos well when confronted by large animals looking for meals, but when the predator is a two thousand-pound steel monster bearing down on them at unnatural speed, choosing that defense all too often results in their demise, for they jump right into the bumper of a car. If

21

instead they knew to hunker down, curl up, and make themselves as small as possible, the chances that the car would travel right over them would greatly improve, and except for a good scare, they could go on doing armadillo things like looking for grubs and insects to eat. Maybe after a few thousand more years of living with human beings, evolution will equip them to choose the right defense mechanism.

Why, you may ask yourself, am I including a lesson in natural science?

Well, I began thinking about what humans do to defend themselves when they are fearful. We also have our defense mechanisms, and choosing the right one might make the difference between diminishing or growing who we are. If we encounter a black bear while hiking in the woods, it might serve us well to wave our arms, shout in our loudest voices, and try to appear bigger than we actually are in hopes of scaring it away. But there is another kind of fear that haunts humans; it results from insecurities arising from daily encounters with ourselves and others. We fear that we aren't as important, smart, right, acceptable, or lovable as we hope we are. These fears won't smash us against the bumper of a car; instead, we might be ridiculed, rejected, or abandoned ... and that can feel much worse.

All too often, we defend ourselves by trying to puff up with words, arguments, or anger in hope of making ourselves appear more than we actually are, or at the very least, shifting the focus somewhere else. Maybe what we really need to do is hunker down, quiet our minds, and identify what our fears are really about. Then we might share honestly what we have learned with another. Allowing ourselves to be vulnerable to others when our biggest fear is that we will be found wanting is what trust is built upon. And love always responds with gentleness, reassurance, and acceptance, because we recognize ourselves in others.

If our vulnerability is met with this kind of love, we become more understood and more secure, and our love stories blossom.

Compassion

One of my childhood friends was the son of the only surgeon in the small town where I grew up. He was one of six sons; all were tall, good-looking, and athletic—destined to become doctors themselves if their mother had any say in it. Needless to say, this family was well-respected, envied by some, and admired by many. My friend was one of the most popular kids in our class.

One day a week during our sixth-grade year, the desks were moved to the perimeter of the classroom, and in lieu of music class, we practiced dancing. As you can imagine, as the girls migrated to one side of the room and the boys the other, there was a lot of tension. For the girls, the ultimate question was, "Will someone ask me to dance?" followed closely by, "Will *he* ask me to dance?" The boys delayed as long as possible, joking with each other (a dead giveaway for discomfort among young males) and talking quietly behind their hands (due to fear of rejection, perhaps) before one brave soul was the first to walk across the expanse of the room and ask some lucky girl to dance.

In contrast to the most popular, handsome boy, there was a girl who came from a very poor rural family. Unfortunately, nature had not blessed her with outward beauty; she was, quite frankly, homely by most standards. And because of her family's poverty, she had no advantage of being able to dress well, have her hair cut stylishly, or have her teeth regularly cleaned. Worse still, she struggled academically. The saying "kids can be cruel" has some real validity, and this young girl suffered from taunts and teasing. She was well aware that her family was shunned. But like every other girl, she was required to present herself as available to dance and stand on the girl's side of the room—by herself.

Every week, the ritual unfolded. But the most popular, handsome boy in that room changed what could have been just another one of the trials young people experience for at least two girls, because every week, he asked the outcast to dance. He took a lot of teasing from his buddies, but he never wavered.

I can't possibly know what that meant to the girl he danced with, but I can tell you that his compassion stuck with me and still touches me fifty years later. I named a son after this childhood friend.

Don't miss opportunities to model this vitally important lesson for others. Kindness and compassion help us to be human—to recognize that none of us gets to choose where we will be placed on this earth. Some of us get very lucky—others, not so much. It's very easy for kids to align with other kids, dividing their peers into in-groups and out-groups as they struggle for their own identity. Teach your children to be compassionate—not out of altruism, but because it's the right thing to do.

Even the outcasts of the world have gifts to share, but they won't be discovered if we don't open ourselves to receiving them.

Our Own Worst Critics

I was twenty years old when my father was diagnosed with lung cancer. In those days, after radiation treatment bought a few more months of life, there wasn't much that could be done to prevent inevitable death. He was only fifty-nine years old—much too young to die.

I am the youngest of my father's five children, and if the older four were closer to Mother, I was his child. He was my champion, my hero, and the one I could always count on to be there for me. I loved trailing after him when I was little, fixing his coffee and running errands for him. My siblings called me his pet, and this name was not always easy to live with.

I began working in the local hospital when I was sixteen. I wanted to be a nurse for as long as I can remember, so it was not surprising that I jumped at the chance to work in the hospital, first as a candy-striper and then eventually as a nurses' aide. At a very young age, I was familiar with illness and death. When my mother made the decision to care for my father at home and surround him with family and friends who loved him rather than subject him to the sterile, regimented care of the hospital, I was the one who was able to take a leave of absence from work and provide some relief for her, even though I no longer worked in the medical field.

By the time I arrived home, my father's condition had deteriorated to the point that he needed assistance in changing positions in the hospital bed set up in our living room. The cancer had progressed to his spine, and although he never complained, he was in a great amount of pain; moving from a supine position to sitting was one of the only means to briefly alleviate that pain. He was too weak to manage that movement by himself.

On a particularly beautiful early summer day, I encouraged my mother to get out of the house. I stayed with Daddy to take care of his needs and she trusted me to do so.

I have been an avid reader since about age five, and I was sitting in the recliner beside my father's bed, reading. He asked me to help him sit up in bed, and I did so. After assuring myself that he was comfortable, I returned to the recliner and had just found my place in the book when he again needed my assistance to change positions.

To my horror, without thought, I made that tongue-clicking sound of impatience and disgust—and my father heard it. He said, "Your old man has become a real pain in the a-- hasn't he?" I was mortified! What kind of daughter was I that I couldn't put my book aside and attend to my dying father?

The shame was overwhelming—not only because family friends declared me to be the compassionate one they knew would help my mother care for my dying father, but also because the man who had cared for, loved, and sacrificed for me heard my impatience.

I didn't share this shame with anyone. I couldn't think about it without tears, and there were many shed privately over the next few years when I visited that terrible day in my mind.

I married, had a couple of beautiful sons, and enjoyed decorating and caring for my first home. Then I began having some bothersome physical problems that were not easily diagnosed. Eventually, I was told that the symptoms I experienced had a psychological origin, and if I didn't figure out what was troubling me, I would be in a mental institution by the time I was thirty! I couldn't believe it; I thought I was a very happy, blessed woman. I couldn't imagine what was troubling me to such a degree—except the one dark secret I had never shared with anyone. I hid the part of me that was selfish, unloving, hateful, and full of shame—the part of me that would put a book and my love of reading above the needs of my dying father, whom I had vowed to care for.

I called my dearest childhood friend, told her I needed to talk, and tearfully drove two hours to her house. Sitting in the rocking chair in her kitchen, I choked out my story and the reason I needed to unburden my heart. I was ready for the punishment I deserved—to hear from someone else all the condemnation I had heaped on myself during the past few years.

Very gently, she said, "Your father was not criticizing or blaming you. He was acknowledging the reality that you both found yourselves in. No father wants to be helpless in the eyes of his child. And no child wants to bear witness to the helplessness of their beloved parent."

I don't think further explanation is necessary. The symptoms I experienced eventually led to a diagnosed physical illness. As painful as this lesson was for me, the message I hope to impart is this: we can be (and often are) our own worst critics. We forget that we are also human and need compassion, both from others and from ourselves. And when we don't know this, we needlessly suffer.

There are many times in the course of life when we do not act the way we would hope to, are not at our best, and move through life mindlessly. There is no shame in acknowledging that fact and forgiving ourselves. I believe we are all trying to do the best we can in the moment with what we are given. It's the best we can do.

I'm Sorry

This is a lesson from many years ago; if I recall correctly, it was a reader's contribution to *Readers' Digest*.

A boy filled out an application for his first job. He came to the question, "What are your strengths?" and he thoughtfully listed what he thought a potential employer might want to hear. He wrote, "I am a good worker, self-motivated, punctual, honest and trustworthy, a fast learner, helpful, considerate of others, and friendly."

The next question was more difficult: "What are your weaknesses?" The boy pondered it for some moments and then wrote, "Sometimes, I am not all of the above."

I think this young man was right on target, for don't we all have moments when we aren't at our best, and are less than honest, sincere, and reliable? We lose energy, get overwhelmed by the daily business of living, forget the impact we have on our loved ones, or don't want to deal with hassles. In other words, we make mistakes. The real question is this: What do we do when we are "not all the above"?

I have heard it said that "I'm sorry" is the most important phrase in a relationship, after "I love you." Sometimes I think those two words are spoken too casually, as if the mere utterance contains some magic. What "I'm sorry" should mean is that you are repentant, remorseful, and regret that you have not presented the best of yourself. When you apologize, you ask for forgiveness.

If your apology is to be meaningful, you must then take responsibility for changing the behavior that you already know has harmed. You have to be mindful enough that the next time you are tempted to be "not all the above," you make a different choice. If you don't, then perhaps what you are really sorry for is being brought to task rather than the offense or hurt you have caused. Perhaps you can be remorseful, but can you be repentant and ask forgiveness? There are no excuses that I can see; we have to accept accountability for our actions.

Don't be afraid to own your mistakes. Don't hesitate to say, "I'm sorry," but do so with a contrite heart and the clear intention of improving your behavior in the future.

Forgiveness

Some of the most important lessons I've learned about love have been learned from my family. When I was a child, I felt that my brother and I were not particularly close and that he preferred his other sisters to me. I wanted his approval all my life but had to grow up a bit (a lot!) to understand that it was always there. The following letters provided the evidence.

When my brother was working abroad, I decided to try to foster a closer relationship than I thought we had had growing up and began corresponding with him.

Dear Jo,

"We were lousy siblings."

"We didn't like each other; we were either hateful or indifferent."

I'm sitting in a hotel room on the other side of the earth and some would consider that fact or the person that created this reality to be special—right? ... In your mind, should I or will I be crushed beneath the judgment ... or are there other considerations? Speaking for myself, I do not feel diminished by the circumstances of my life, and in fact, I must admit the opposite is the case. I'm saying that we *must* realize that no matter how clear our images of the past might be, they are only images. Every detail has been processed by our beliefs, our defense mechanisms, our minds—and the image is *not* the truth. The windows through which we preserve the world are truly limited, and often our willing judgment of ourselves and others narrows our perspective even more.

We weren't "lousy" siblings, Jo; we were people experiencing the full range of emotions associated with all true relationships. Included in that range was indifference, admiration, respect, hate, and most important of all, love. Once love has been experienced by two people, it's not given up; even when we think it was unjustified, unreasonable, or unhealthy, it lingers on. I don't think love is about making decisions based on consideration—or about choice, for that matter. Love seems to be a spiritual connection. So perhaps you have "thought about, stewed about, and cried about our relationship long enough."

There is a difference between needing and wanting and a difference between wanting and needing and loving. We all have a right to what we need but not necessarily to what we want, so what about loving? Isn't love what we need or what we want? Isn't it something to work, barter, win for? I mean to ask you if you're stewing about what you need or what you want—do you have expectations, and are you disappointed when your wishes are not realized?

I mean to tell you, Jo, that I need and want your love. I mean to tell you that I need and want your admiration and respect. I mean to tell you that you have my admiration and respect as well as my love without consideration or choice. I'm for you, because I'm for you. "The last couple of years, I've really wished that I would have gone to college right after high school, simply because it's so boring to spend a third of your life doing something pretty insignificant." What about what you have to offer the world?

"I still feel that my family is the greater of my obligations and responsibilities and worth making my highest priority, but there are days that I really hate what I've done." And there are women in the struggle who would envy you—so what is important is to realize that when we have one thing, we will always wish for the other. I mean to tell you that I'm for you—no expectations, just expectancy and true joy when we are able to connect. Your greatest obligation and responsibility is to yourself—realizing your own potential as a human being, and in doing so, you will contribute to the self-actualization of those you hold most dear. It needn't really be a choice between "being a free woman who's alone more than she chooses, and a vassal exhausted by the demands of others who never guess that she has needs herself." There is a price—there is always a price—and the struggle will enhance the reward or increase the value ...

That moment one definitely commits oneself, then Providence moves too. All sorts of things occur to help one that would never otherwise have occurred. A whole stream of events issues from the decision, raising in one's favor all manner of unforeseen incidents and meetings and material assistance, which no man or woman could have dreamed would have come his or her way.

Whatever you can do, or dreamed you can do, begin it. Boldness has genius, power and magic in it. Begin it now. (Goethe, 1749–1832)

So there you have it. Not much more to say, really, except that time and distance makes this all a little impersonal for me. That's not to say it's not heartfelt as much as it's a comment on how little we share in terms of our day-to-day ups and downs. That's reality, but there are times I wish it weren't so.

Love always,

Your Only Brother

I'm ashamed that when I received the above letter, I somehow missed all the love it contained, and it infuriated me! I responded by saying that I didn't feel I ever had a brother, managed without one for all the years of my life thus far, and was willing to let sleeping dogs lie, so to speak.

It wasn't until some months later that I wanted the quote from Goethe and remembered that it was contained in *that letter* from my brother. I scrounged around in my correspondence and reread his letter. I was baffled! What had made me so angry upon first reading? Where was my head and, more importantly, my heart? I don't know. At least I had the courage to tell him that I had erred and treated him badly. I wrote again with apology and humility. To that, he responded,

Dear Sister,

Do you ever read Ann Landers or *Dear Abby?* It seems to me that those two women have been earning a living stating the obvious. Most folks are doing the best they can with the cards they've been dealt (every day). Is there ever any justification for doing anything less? I'm sure glad fate handed us a new deck, and it should be clear I don't need any apology. You've got to know from your experience that two people never see the same events from the same perspective. Your reevaluation of an old letter makes it easy to see that time tends to move us all around more than just a little.

I was glad that you let your sense of humor shine a bit—"could have been a test" "You could just think of me as your slow sister." Nobody has the upper hand in my book. Seeing what's going on and enjoying it is about all any of us can really do. I mean to say, there are no axes to grind, no explanations required. I've missed you, and there is some catching up to do on your journey since Texas. The Japanese Law of Bushido says one "must anticipate nothing but one must also be prepared for anything." So let's adopt an Eastern point of view. It's time to have some fun again.

Love always,

Your Only Brother

What incredible forgiveness! What love! It was the beginning—no, the realization—of one of the most important relationships of my life. Listen to the message. Our own perceptions flavor the other's intentions more than we can possibly imagine. Think carefully about this lesson.

I hope you can see that these are more than letters between me and my brother. There are real lessons about love and forgiveness contained within. I love this man! He is truly one of my life's gifts, and I wanted you to benefit from his wisdom.

My brother has taught me much about the love story. I pass it on to you.

Happiness

A common plea seems to be "I just want to be happy."
Happiness is just one of the multitude of emotions we have in our repertoire. It is not the ultimate goal—any more than sadness, disappointment, elation, or excitement. If, indeed, we had a steady diet of any of those emotions, we would be exhausted, and eventually, we would become immune to the experience of that emotion.

If you are one of those individuals who just wants everyone to be happy, I ask you, why? If we want people to experience the world as fully as possible—unfortunately with all its pain, and thankfully with all its joy—would you still wish for someone to be happy all the time?

We are hedonistic by nature. When things go well, we are usually very content to keep them that way and avoid rocking the boat if at all possible. When we are faced with difficulties and challenges—when we *aren't* particularly happy—we test our true mettle. When we meet a challenge, we grow in our feelings of competency and confidence. If we consider this carefully, wouldn't we want everyone to grow into his or her full potential, even if it means that person is not always happy?

Harder yet is the realization that we have no power to make another person happy—even those we love most dearly. The choice to be happy is up to each person. As one friend reminded me, "People are about as happy as they decide to be."

Of course, if there are no moments of happiness in your life, then something needs to be addressed, and I encourage you to do so. Life lived in a continual state of dissatisfaction, hurt, and conflict is no life to be cherished. But don't worry too much if you and your loved ones aren't in a continual state of happiness. Life has many ups and downs. There is joy but also pain. Try not to worry too much about it. It's out of our hands anyway, and I've come to realize that life's painful trials eventually pass. With time and retrospection, we may find a deeper understanding of who we are and what we can surmount even if we can't appreciate it in the moment of anguish.

I would hope that people strive more for contentment than happiness. If when you lay your head on the pillow each night, you can review your day and acknowledge all that it presented to you, examine how you met challenges as well as pleasures, and know when you have presented your best, then you can sigh, "I'm content." That's about as good as it gets.

Laughter and Tears

I t may appear odd that I group these two seemingly disparate behaviors together, but they have some interesting similarities.

Do you know that humans are the only creatures who can either laugh or cry? Other animals have tear glands, but they are only used to moisten the eye. And although dogs and other animals appear to show their pleasure through behaviors such as tail wagging, you'll never hear another creature laugh.

So what might the purpose of laughter and tears be? My hunch is that our Creator gave them to us—along with the power to think and feel a full range of emotions—knowing we would need some kind of release valve in the same manner a pressure cooker needs a pressure regulator to prevent it from exploding. Support for this comes from research that shows that tears shed in sadness have a different chemical composition than those that come when peeling onions or after slamming a finger in a door. Emotional tears contain the same chemicals that are present in the body when under stress and are likely the body's means to eliminate some of these powerful hormones.

People often say, "I don't want to cry," and my response is frequently, "Why not?" Forget about what you were taught about "sucking it up," and think about the release you feel after a good cry. After the snotty nose and sense that it will never stop, there is a feeling of letting go. Don't we feel better after a good cry?

Like tears, laughter seems to help keep us centered and prevents us from becoming needlessly serious or self-absorbed. Some people have a great sense of humor and are quicker to find the humor in life than others; I treasure friends who inspire me to be less serious than is my nature.

Laughter is good for our souls. Its sounds and body mechanics are kind of ridiculous, but think about the last good belly laugh you had—when you laughed until you felt the muscles in your stomach ache and the tears roll down your cheeks. What a sensational feeling! Being silly, telling jokes, and enjoying comedy wherever you can find it ease the tension and change your mood.

I recall green farts and gas attacks when my boys were young. Gales of laughter enveloped the family when the two were feeding off one another in good adolescent humor. They still bring a smile thirty years later when one of us mentions such silliness. Humor must be something of value if it hangs around for so long, don't you think?

Let go, laugh, and cry when you need to. Laughter and tears are gifts. Accept them.

Sex

Wow! *S*, *E*, and *X* are three powerful little letters! Strung together in that particular order, they can conjure up a range of emotions. I realize that this particular subject can be difficult for many people. But in my counseling experience the three areas that cause the most difficulty in marriages are money, sex, and children and talking candidly about any of these topics might help mitigate future problems.

I believe that sex is a gift and should be respected as such. Engagement in the sexual act for purposes other than procreation sets us apart from the rest of God's creatures. Sex can be a playful quickie full of laughter, a soul-deep, intimate connection, or anything in between. There are two things, however, that I hope you remember.

First, there is a natural ebb and flow of sexual desire. Don't become alarmed. Hopefully, you and your partner will be in sync most of the time, but when you're not, be patient and understanding. Periods of abstinence won't hurt you; sublimate that energy into cleaning the house, exercising, or distracting yourself in a healthy way. Don't take your partner's occasional disinterest personally. (If, however, you frequently feel rejected or punished there may be problems that need to be discussed and resolved. In that case, commit yourself to doing so.)

Second, intimacy should not be withheld or used in a manipulative way. It can bring you close and give contentedness that lasts for hours, or it can be a weapon that drives you apart and makes one or both of you feel less than desirable, hurt, or confused. There is a definite difference between not being in a receptive state (either physically or emotionally) and withholding to punish the other.

I think our society has damaged the true beauty of sexuality by using it to hawk everything from toothpaste to the cars we drive. I also hear repeatedly of online infidelity that is just a keystroke away but is every bit as hurtful and damaging to trust as the motel trysts of old, even though those who partake would like to deny it.

I am well aware that there are many agreed-upon styles of marriage, including open marriages, in which this most intimate act is knowingly shared. I've never heard of an open relationship working well for very long; it's pretty hard to bring others into your relationship in that way and maintain the commitment that is made between partners. In my way of thinking, good marriages are based on true friendship and deep intimacy. We can share friendship with many; be cautious about sharing sexual intimacy, even in talk.

I have witnessed the embarrassment and pain on the face of a spouse as he listened, along with a roomful of friends, to a partner share bedroom intimacies at a party. I guess his partner attempted to be entertaining. I found her speech contemptuous.

If you have ongoing sexual difficulties, I encourage you to get professional advice. Many are trained to help couples develop a more satisfying sexual union; just make sure you're consulting a licensed professional.

I Am Very Angry

How did we get to be such an angry society? It's evident everywhere, reported in incidences ranging from shootings and tragic death to road rage. Anger management classes are mandated by the courts and suggested by therapists. In counseling, anger is so often identified as the presenting problem that I believe many who do not seek professional help deal with it on their own, even though it does not reach newsworthy status. I hope my own thoughts about anger provide food for thought for those who are seen as angry people, because anger can be very detrimental to health as well as relationships.

Anger is just one of numerous emotions. It is neither good nor bad; it is simply another transient feeling. I think of it as the psyche's equivalent of pain in the physiological world. Pain tells us that we best remove our hand from the fire, because we are causing damage to tissue. Anger tells us that we perceive something wrong in our emotional world and is related to one's interpretation of being offended, wronged, or denied and a tendency to react through retaliation. The Encarta English Dictionary defines anger as "a normal emotion that involves a strong uncomfortable and emotional response to a perceived provocation." I believe that it often masks what is really at the heart of our emotional pain.

Because we put good or bad connotations to our emotions—we like the good feeling, happiness, and don't like feeling bad emotions like disappointment—anger has become a demon. In the recent past, society allowed males to express anger but regarded feelings of hurt, fear, or sadness as not masculine and encouraged females to feel all the above except anger, which was considered to be unfeminine. Females could cry; males could not. Hopefully, we have become wiser in our understanding of emotion and its purpose in life.

The truth is that we all experience the full range of feelings, including anger. Problems arise with inappropriate expression of our emotions—not only in our relationships and society in general, but also for our own self-esteem and physical health.

The reaction to our feelings is what we allow others to witness, and therefore, may provide a protective factor. Anger can be used to keep others from getting too close to us. It may give a sense of power, especially because a very angry outburst stimulates the fight-or-flight response and is accompanied by a surge of adrenaline. (I counseled a person who struggled with anger most of his life and admits that after an intense angry outburst, he feels a sense of incredible release.) Regularly responding with anger to events or interactions that displease us can become habit and also allows one to ignore personal responsibility; there is no need for introspection if we blame the other: "He (she) *makes* me so angry ..."

When you feel anger start to surface, take a deep breath, remind yourself that emotions are transient and have a message to impart, and ask yourself, "What about this situation makes me so angry?" The anger may be caused by a feeling of rejection, hurt, or fear (that you will be found wanting in some way and therefore rejected or criticized). It may be caused by disappointment, frustration, or being taken advantage of—emotion that reflects on you in what you perceive to be a negative way. It is necessary to peel back the anger in order to access the emotion that is more difficult to look at. If the underlying feeling is not identified, it is almost impossible to resolve what is at the core of the distress; therefore, the angry habit continues. Think about the following scenario, which occurred at a forensic facility in which I worked.

The inmates were required to line up in a predetermined order in the hallway so they could be escorted as a group to the "chow hall." This entailed walking down stairs and through a rather heavy fire door that separated the unit from the hallway.

One of the inmates I met with after the midday meal was becoming increasingly angry with another inmate. He said little about the problem but spent the majority of our time together making derogatory statements about the man who had become his tormentor. Our sessions were derailed, because talking about his angry demeanor without finding the answer to the question, "What is making you so angry?" was fairly unproductive.

After a few weeks, he was involved in a physical altercation with the man who preceded him in the cafeteria line each day. His anger finally boiled over, and because there were serious repercussions for fighting and he wanted to deflect some of the blame, he was more motivated to explore the cause of his anger, even if it meant giving up some of his tough-guy demeanor and risking vulnerability.

Every day, the other inmate let the door close just as this man reached the bottom of the stairs, and very often, it seemed to slam right in his face. This *made him mad!* It took some time for my client to discover that under his anger was a feeling of being disrespected. He felt invisible to the other—not even important enough to hold a door open for. He remembered all the times, beginning in childhood, when he was belittled, insulted, or ignored by his father—when he felt disrespected. It was a real revelation for him to see that long-standing hurt still directed his behavior. Finally, some healing could begin!

Not insignificantly, when we finally brought the offender into a session and my client told him what he was struggling with, the response was immediate. The offender said something like, "Gee, man, I'm sorry. I never thought about holding the door." My client realized he wasn't being disrespected; rather, his peer had bad manners! From that point on, the door was always held open.

I like what is taught in the following passage, known only as an old Cherokee parable.

An old Cherokee chief was teaching his grandson about life. "A fight is going on inside me," he said to the boy. "It is a terrible fight, and it is between two wolves. One is evil—he is anger, envy, sorrow, regret, greed, arrogance, self-pity, guilt, resentment, inferiority, lies, false pride, superiority, self-doubt, and ego. The other is good—he is joy, peace, love, hope, serenity, humility, kindness, benevolence, empathy, generosity, truth, compassion, and faith. This same fight is going on inside you—and inside every other person, too."

The grandson thought about it for a minute and then asked his grandfather, "Which wolf will win?"

The old chief simply replied, "The one you feed."

—Author Unknown

If we want to feed the good, we have to identify the evil that may take root in our hearts. It's not enough to just be angry. Ask "Why?" The reward is higher self-esteem, peace, and better health—both personally and in your relationships.

The Inevitable

No matter how we may resist this fact, life is dynamic. It is full of change, and the unforeseeable is the cause of the generalized anxiety that overwhelms many of us. Anxiety, according to the Merriam-Webster Dictionary, is a painful uneasiness of mind, usually over an impending or anticipated ill; an overwhelming sense of fear often marked by doubt concerning the reality and nature of the threat and self-doubt about one's capacity to cope with it.

I believe self-doubt about one's capacity to cope causes most of our distress and intensifies a tendency to want to cling to that with which we are familiar, even as change occurs.

Three women come to mind when I think about this easily-assumed state of mind. All of them have experienced great difficulties in their lives; two faced serious illness, both personally and of loved ones; two were in abusive relationships that became life-threatening; one lost her livelihood, a thriving business she created and loved, to an arsonist; all have grieved the loss of loved ones. But all three remain upbeat, joyful people who are apparently able to rebound from those serious setbacks with remarkable speed. What they display is resiliency—an ability to recover from or adjust to misfortune or change. I asked them if they could explain.

One said that she allowed herself to grieve her loss—whether it was of health, resources, or a loved one—but did not allow herself to get stuck in grieving. After two or three days, she refocuses on what she still has, and that is what she builds upon. Poignantly, she gave the example of discovering that her oldest, beloved grandson was diagnosed with an affliction for which there is no cure. After she cried for the little boy, his parents, and herself, she reminded herself that it could be worse. The illness was not life-threatening, and there was hope that as he matured, the symptoms would diminish. Although there would be challenges, her grandson was still the wonderful, talented, beautiful little boy that he had always been. She educated herself about the illness so that fear will be unable to feed off ignorance and get a grip on her spirit.

Another related that bad things just don't seem to stick in her mind. She does whatever she is able to do to ameliorate the problem and then moves on as quickly as possible. She uses her many talents to explore the possibilities still open to her and immerses herself in the comforts she has spent a lifetime creating.

The third remembered exactly what enabled her to become more resilient—a conscious choice. She related a marriage gone terribly wrong; along with her husband's increasing dependency on alcohol came increasingly frightening physical abuse. With three small children to protect, she knew she had to get out of the relationship when he began threatening her life. She had no means of support or place to live. The next years were difficult. She relied on family to help with the children as she reordered her life. She enrolled in college, worked to pay the bills, and became the solitary head of household. Her ex-husband did not contribute with child support, and worse, he violated the restraining order granted by the courts and continued to stalk and threaten her.

She said her life was full of worry. She would lie awake at night, worrying whether she would be able to pay both the electric bill and buy groceries. She worried about her children and whether they were receiving all the nurturing they needed; the lack of time she had to study to get grades good enough to graduate; her ability to keep up the pace of work, study, and mothering; and whether her ex-husband would carry out his threats. She was exhausted.

Then late one night, unable to sleep, she realized that all of her worry made absolutely no difference in the outcome of any of her problems. She reminded herself that she was managing; things got done, and she was moving toward her goals and a better life for her children and herself. Worrying did not contribute to her success but robbed her of rest and energy her days required. She also had a clear realization that when confronted with the immediacy of a problem, somehow the solution appeared.

With that, she decided to no longer allow herself to worry. If worry began to rear its ugly head, she reminded herself of her new commitment. Now, years later, remarried with almost-grown children, she admits that she seldom gets too upset about life's problems. ("And that was probably a very good thing, considering life with four teenage daughters!" she laughingly adds.) Her husband sometimes gets frustrated with what he believes to be her Pollyanish attitude, attributing it to a lack of caring. But she has learned she is capable of meeting life's challenges and trusts she will be okay.

I know all of these women well and can attest to the fact that they feel deeply and experience the same disappointments, frustrations, and concerns that plague us all. I think they have developed a high degree of resilience that is innate in all of us to some degree.

Resilience is not invulnerability but rather the capacity to rise above difficult circumstances. It is a trait that allows us to exist in this less-than-perfect world while moving forward with optimism and confidence, even in the midst of adversity.

Too often, we find ourselves imagining the worst to come. If unemployed, we fear that we won't find fulfilling work; if experiencing physical ailments, we fear that a catastrophic illness is lurking in the body; if mourning the end of a relationship, we fear that we'll never find a partner with whom to share a meaningful life. Each of these examples can cause anxiety to flourish. Take a moment to ask yourself, "Is there evidence to support this fear, or am I trusting my crystal ball of catastrophe?"

If a fear is evidence-based, do what you can to address the problem. Update your resume, and begin networking with your friends and acquaintances. Get to the doctor. Recognize that your relationship had characteristics and flaws that could not be ignored and wasn't meant to be. Know that your soul mate will have a better chance of appearing in your life if you don't isolate yourself but instead use every opportunity to let your love light shine.

Life gives us our share of suffering. Don't subject yourself to it unnecessarily by imagining what might not ever occur. Don't borrow trouble.

Don't Defeat Yourself

The fourth decade of my life was particularly difficult. What I thought was a stable, twenty-year marriage began to unravel as my husband and I drifted further and further apart. Our sons were beginning their own lives away from home, and without work I found valuable or challenging, my life felt shallow and dissatisfying. I was depressed.

After weeks of counseling, my therapist asked me what I intended to do to create a more acceptable life for myself. I had already contemplated this question and could readily answer, "I might have become a psychologist at one time, but that's no longer an option."

"Why not?" my therapist asked.

"Because I don't even have an undergraduate degree, and with the six years of graduate school on top of that, I'll be fifty before I can even begin to practice."

What my therapist said next was one of the most important, life-changing lessons I had yet to learn. "Jo, you are thinking about this wrong. Hopefully, you will become fifty no matter what you do. The choice is this: you will either arrive at your fiftieth year and say with regret, 'If I would have started back then, I would have had my degree now,' or you will joyfully exclaim, 'I've made it! I can now begin my career as a psychologist!'"

Like all good counseling, those words offered a perspective that had not occurred to me. Needless to say, I chose the second option and have had the satisfaction of helping people through their life challenges for the past fourteen years. My career has taken me to places I never dreamed of working—with folks in prisons, hospitals, and the military.

I won't mislead you by saying it was easy. I gave up many of the comforts my marriage had provided and often felt alone on my new journey of hard work and challenging tasks. There were times I felt like quitting and those who encouraged me to do so, thinking I had finally come to my senses. But I was also blessed to have others in my life who encouraged me not to give up and reminded me of the goal I was working to attain. Without hesitation, I can tell you that the rewards far exceed the sacrifice.

How often do we defeat ourselves by being afraid of the unknown, uncertain if we can meet the challenges, or discouraged by setbacks along the way? How many of us are trapped in unfulfilling circumstances, letting our dreams wither and die, because our inner, fear-driven voices say, "I can't"? How often do we listen to the counsel of others who have less than our best interest at heart?

Read again Goethe's advice that was shared with me in my brother's letter many years ago: "Whatever you can do, or dreamed you can do, begin it. Boldness has genius, power and magic in it. Begin it now."

Resentment

Much of this book addresses the emotional life that we all experience and I encourage you to embrace. I will warn you against just one emotion—resentment. It imprisons the soul. It is the offspring of anger and the perceived or real injustices we suffer. Some people let one, two, or maybe ten unpleasant experiences poison the rest of their lives. They let their anger turn to bitterness until they end up seeing themselves as victims of their parents, their peers, and even the time into which they were born. Sadly, there are truly unhappy people who seek to hurt and humiliate—who want to trap others in that prison of anger and resentment. Do not fall into the trap.

My World Might Not Look Like Yours

Are you familiar with this picture of the old, almost witch-y looking, woman with a big nose (complete with wart) and pointed chin? She's wearing a babushka and is peering down from little eyes. Wait! That's not an old woman! It's a young, rather elegant woman looking over her shoulder. She has a feather in her hat and perhaps a fur around her shoulders. Well, which one is it?

It doesn't matter which one you saw first; either one is correct. Some flexible people can easily see both and flip back and forth depending upon which one they want to see. Others need the opposite pointed out to them before they can see her. This is a lesson in perception.

We live in a world that is not made of hard facts and reality but presents itself to each of us sifted through the personal filters we have developed since childhood. We become attuned to certain aspects of the presented world. This may contribute to the reason a number of people witnessing the same event describe it differently.

Trouble arises when we attribute our perceptions to others and assume they see the world in the same manner we do. We might take this a step further and compound our error by thinking we know the motivation of another or by attributing a personality characteristic (usually for a behavior we have witnessed and find unacceptable).

Try a little exercise to prove this point. Imagine that you are driving in your car and are just about to enter a fairly busy highway. You begin to merge into traffic when another driver appears out of nowhere and cuts you off. He's driving much too fast, and as you watch him, you notice him weaving in and out of traffic as he races down the highway.

You feel your pulse quicken and blood pressure rise. If you hadn't been driving defensively, that jerk most likely would have sideswiped you! As your internal dialogue continues, you perceive that you have just encountered a selfish, irresponsible, careless fool—a threat to law-abiding citizens just trying to get to their destination. You may even be tempted to try to catch up to him and give him a taste of his own medicine.

Can you imagine yourself in this scenario and feel your body respond? Can you identify with a similar situation in your own life?

Everything you've witnessed stays the same. The only change occurs in the attributions you make about the driver of that car, for you now have the ability to *know* what is behind that careless idiot's behavior. Let's see if it changes your perception of him.

The man was sitting at his desk, just another day at work, when he received a call from an emergency room doctor notifying him that his little boy was badly injured in an accident and in need of immediate surgery. He had to get to the hospital as soon as possible to sign consent papers and possibly donate blood.

Does that story change your thoughts about him and his erratic behavior? Are you more apt to say a prayer for his safe arrival and the recovery of his child? Would you act similarly in his shoes?

This story is a pretty dramatic example, but I wanted to make a point. We never know what is happening in another's life (unless he or she shares it with us). All the anger you might have experienced in this little experiment occurred inside you and harmed no one but yourself.

We do this more often than we might think. The husband isn't home at the time he promised, because he can't be trusted to keep his word. A friend doesn't show up when expected, because he or she doesn't really care about your feelings. Isn't it better to give the other the benefit of the doubt or simply acknowledge that everyone—including you—gets distracted, loses track of time, and acts less than favorably?

Be careful when judging the motivations of another. Chances are pretty good that you might be mistaken.

I Just Don't Want to Fight Anymore

I don't blame you. Fighting is hurtful and energy-zapping and too often ends in stalemate, anyway. I do not, however, advocate the avoidance of conflict. We are not clones of one another and will have differences of opinion, perspective, and desire.

How we approach conflict determines whether or not there is a chance for resolution after both parties feel heard, have an opportunity to try to persuade the other to their point of view, and come to some point in negotiating a settlement that satisfies the needs of both to at least some degree.

First, each party must be willing to respectfully listen to the other's point of view. Listening doesn't mean you agree; it simply means you are willing to hear the other person out. In essence, you are saying, "I am interested in you and want to hear your point of view on this subject. I am willing to keep a rein on my opinion until you are finished." You must actively listen, giving all your attention to the other. Then, of course, the other respectfully reciprocates. Only when both parties feel they have been heard is it appropriate to move on.

During the phase of persuasion, each attempts to move the other closer to his or her point of view: "I feel … because …." There are, of course, no guarantees of success here, but if both parties are interested in finding a reasonable resolution, they will try hard to be open to conceding points that, upon further explanation, they might agree to.

The final phase of negotiation is about finding a compromise that respects the feelings of both parties. Both must work cooperatively to find middle ground on which each person feels he or she can live comfortably. In essence, compromise is working toward a win-win situation.

With the above information, it's time for some introspection. If you find that you are frequently in conflict, can you recognize the area that causes the most difficulty? Since you know that you are only responsible for yourself, look for ways that you might contribute to the problem.

Perhaps you frequently interrupt or show some sign of disrespect while the other voices his or her opinions. Perhaps you show that you are not really interested in what is being said but are waiting impatiently for the conclusion so you can state what is really important!

Perhaps you contribute by trying to out-shout the other, bullying your partner into hearing you. Maybe you try to intimidate by name-calling or implying that the other doesn't know what he or she is talking about.

Perhaps you sulk, answering "What's wrong?" with "Nothing." If the question was asked, it must appear that something is amiss. Silence or non-response should not be an option. If, however, you feel yourself too emotionally invested in the moment, claim it: "I'm really too upset to talk about this right now. But I do want to figure it out. Can you give me some time so I can calm myself and be more clear-headed?" Ask for the time, but promise yourself and your partner that you *will* return to the discussion. This also means there is no storming away, slamming the door behind you, leaving your partner wondering where you have gone and when (or if) you will be back. That is abandonment, and it only adds fuel to the fire.

Do you insist on getting your own way? That's an error in the third phase of compromise and is unlikely to resolve a conflict. It may provide an escape for the present, but it's likely that the same issue will surface again.

Discuss the problem at hand, not the grievances you harbor from the past. In fact, if you find yourself in a relationship in which the same quarrels repeat over and over, my hunch is that the process is short-circuited before resolution is ever reached. Perhaps you apologize just to end the fight.

It is very hard to think of these things in the moment of heightened emotion, so take time to think about what you want and how you can best work toward getting it during quiet alone time. Become a good negotiator; it will serve you in many arenas.

If He Really Loved Me

I s this a statement you've ever made? Do you expect that your partner is so in tune with you that he or she can read your mind? I learned an important lesson from a Native American women's retreat that I (one of only two Caucasian women) was invited to attend.

The retreat weekend was incredible! About fifty women from all over the United States and Central America were at this retreat. No men were allowed except those needed to prepare fantastic meals for us and care for the small number of children who were brought along. For the most part, it wasn't even evident they were there.

The weekend was designed to remind us of important lessons that would normally be passed down from the elders. It began with a sweat, a powerful cleansing ceremony, and ended with the event I share with you now.

After two full days of interaction with these women, I wanted nothing more than to please those around me and be remembered as a woman of like mind and spirit. We entered the main hall of the ashram where we were staying and were delighted to see a buffet set before us that could have rivaled any seen in the finest hotel. The theme was Southwestern; everything made from scratch, including the refried beans (a favorite of mine and made the authentic way). There were homemade tortillas, carna asada, rice—too much to mention.

As we entered the room, we were asked only one question: "Do you have allergies to any of the foods presented here?" (No one did). Then we were instructed to find a woman with whom we had had little interaction during the weekend and felt we didn't know well. We paired up before moving to the buffet table.

Next, we each were to fix the plate of the woman with whom we were paired. We were not to talk. We could not ask if our partner liked a particular dish, how hungry she was, whether she preferred tea (sweetened or unsweetened? lemon or not?) or water with her meal. And then we went to a table.

The next instruction was to feed our partner what we had selected for her. We were not allowed to talk or give any indication whether we liked what was put on our plates and into our mouths, how quickly we preferred to eat, or whether we would like a sip of water between bites. It was totally up to the "feeder" to figure that out.

Keep in mind that we all, I believe, wanted to please—wanted our last experience with one another to be a memorable one. This was one difficult task! I know that I felt some confusion but a deep desire to "do it right."

After the meal was finished, we were asked for responses to what we experienced. I recall that every woman began by turning to her partner and saying something like, "I hope that was okay.

Did I choose the right foods? Did I feed you too fast?" (I would have preferred more refried beans!)

The point of the exercise was this: no matter how you want to please or how good your intentions, you cannot know what pleases the other without his or her input.

You may think you know another person well—and sometimes you do. But what might please one moment may change in the next, influenced by mood, level of fatigue, and numerous other factors. If you really want to know how to please another, ask! Our intentions are filtered through our own desires and perspective, and that is not necessarily the other's.

Don't assume that your beloved will know how to please you if he or she loves you. Love doesn't bestow mind-reading, no matter how much we would like that to be true. Be willing to share your desire.

Lemon Pie

Lemon meringue pie is a family favorite; none liked it more than our mother. I learned from a very early age that it was her favorite dessert; this was something we had in common.

Children grow up and establish their own households, and parents' life circumstances change as well. So it was with my family. My siblings and I moved, married, and scattered across the country. After our father's death, Mother left our family home in Michigan to create a new life for herself in Florida. She was an independent woman with a strong sense of adventure and curiosity, so it was not surprising when she bought a motor home to satisfy what she called the gypsy in her. Of course, the downside of all this movement was infrequent opportunities for us to share with one another; our visits became limited to three or four each year.

Somewhere along the way, I decided that I would make lemon pie for Mother every time I had the opportunity to see her. If I was the one traveling to her, I brought a pie along as my little house gift. If she stopped in her motor home on her way to some distant state, I made sure there was a lemon pie in the small refrigerator for her journey.

Every time I rolled the crust, stirred the filling until it thickened into tart, lemony goodness, or heaped the meringue into clouds of sweetness, I thought of Mother and envisioned her enjoying the confection I made for her. Unlike times when the whole family was together and she was lucky to get just one small piece, she could have the whole thing to herself! Even when I didn't find time to make the pie until after children were asleep and other chores were done, I made sure the pie was ready before I went to bed.

After this ritual went on for a couple of years, there was an occasion when mother was with me for a few days, and pie-baking had to wait until the night before her departure so it would be fresh. As I got out the ingredients, she said to me, "Honey, your pies taste like cornstarch, because you don't cook the lemon filling slowly and long enough!"

"Mother! Why has it taken you so long to tell me?" I cried.

My mother replied, "I didn't want to hurt your feelings."

I was hurt—not because I didn't make a stellar lemon pie (perhaps I was more embarrassed by that), but because I was uncertain whether I could trust that Mother knew me well enough to know that I could accept feedback without offense and was open to learning.

Mother was a very kind person who would rather eat a dozen cornstarch-tasting pies than risk hurting my feelings. But in her sensitivity to others, she committed a grave error: she tried to take responsibility for my feelings. I was left wondering why it is so difficult to share our observations or experiences if they are less than ideal—even with those we love.

Perhaps we become uncertain how to deliver constructive criticism. That's not surprising, since *criticism* means judgment of what is wrong or bad or disapproval that points out our faults. If we feel disapproval, it doesn't hurt less because "constructive" precedes it. That simply implies positive or useful disapproval. How might we share our less-than-favorable observations so that the recipient remains open to receiving the feedback? I think the answer lies in how we deliver the message.

"Honey, I really appreciate your thoughtfulness. It's a wonderful way to stay connected with you as I roam about the country. But I've noticed that your pie filling needs to cook over lower heat, even if it takes a bit longer to thicken, to rid it of that cornstarchy taste. I think if you try that, you will become an expert at making a *really* good lemon pie."

I would have preferred to get this message much sooner, if not after the first pie (maybe just an unfortunate fluke)—certainly after the second. It could have been a lovely mother-daughter teaching moment to improve my skills so that the real thing was as good as what I had intended. I'm sure *she* would have been more pleased with yet another lemon pie!

Be gentle in sharing your experience if it might be hurtful to hear, but do share it! Be clear about what you are critiquing. As the recipient, try not to take criticism personally. If it is not a judgment about your character, see the opportunity to grow, both in skill and closeness to your teacher.

When Is Enough Enough?

There is a coffee table book entitled *Life at Home in the Twenty-First Century*,[1] a recent anthropological study of thirty-two middle-class American families that records the obscene quantities of stuff that we are buried in. It is full of pictures of freezers packed with prefab food, avalanches of clothes, and towers of molded plastic in bright primary colors.

One of the book's most interesting facts is that the United States has 3.1 percent of the world's children but buys 40 percent of all toys sold worldwide. Those who buy all these goodies know that many of these toys are given a cursory glance and a one-time attempt to entertain; few of them stimulate the imagination or become a favorite plaything. In fact, many end up piled on shelves or shut away in closets to be weeded out (often at Christmastime) to make room for the newest batch of things that children just can't live without and adults can't resist providing. The complaint, "I'm bored. I don't have anything to do" is still heard.

Of course, toys are not our only obsession. We buy too much of everything, whether it's the newest electronic gizmo; another pair of shoes, jeans, or shorts; or any of the consumer goods too numerous to mention. We even entertain ourselves with television programs about hoarders—those poor folks who have lost all sense of personal value and try to fill the void with stuff.

I'm not suggesting that we all have developed a serious obsessive mental disorder. But on a smaller scale, I think we all might take a second look and re-evaluate our level of consumerism.

We are offered a plethora of goods that marketers encourage us to buy even though our nation's credit debt is enormous and our savings in comparison are inadequate. In a capitalistic society, this is the only way to keep people employed; they produce the goods for sale to keep the economy growing. But who benefits? It is not the person who believes that value is based on possession.

I believe this to be true simply by looking at the facts. Americans are the most overweight and obese people that the world has ever seen. As previously noted, we have incredibly high rates of depression and anxiety (indeed, all mental illness). It seems to me that we are trying hard to fill the inner discomfort with stuff, be it food, toys, clothes, or cell phones ... and it doesn't work.

I like the saying, "God put man on earth to love one another and use things, but some get this confused." Don't be one of the confused. Think carefully before you make your next purchase, and ask yourself if you are buying it because you need it, if you have the discretionary funds to purchase it, or if you are trying to fill a void (loneliness or boredom, for example). If the latter is the case, purchasing a new gadget seldom provides more than a momentary lift of the spirit. Find a more appropriate remedy.

Wanting to keep up with the Joneses is a treadmill you don't want to get on. If you're already running, make the conscious decision to stop. Despite what the media would have you believe, you will not be happier, sexier, or in any way more desirable because you are seen with the most recent trend.

It seems to me that huge malls are designed to be the new playground for consumers. They certainly have appealing visual stimulation, good smells from cookie or pretzel kiosks, and comfortable seating where we can enjoy our lattes and take it all in—every aspect necessary to engage the senses. Assuredly, I am not the only one aware of this.

How lasting is the pleasure? Are we really just bored? Think about it. There's a better way to find contentment.

When we love,
we always strive to be better than we are.
When we strive to be better than we are,
everything around us becomes better, too.

—Paulo Caelho, *The Alchemist*

The Beauty of Diversity

Have you ever stood before a well-planned garden and marveled at how it delighted the eye? A beautiful garden is not homogeneous. Perhaps your eye is first drawn to the slender stalks of a grouping of yellow snapdragons, covered with small, individual flowers; directly below them are first cousins: dwarf snapdragons in white. Off to the side is a grouping of deep red zinnias (with a visiting white snapdragon or two). These are big, bold flowers with jagged green leaves that enhance their color perfectly. Lobelia are clear, true blue, small flowers that might not be noticed if they weren't huddled together in such a mass, their cool blue needed as relief from the warmth of the yellows and reds. Scattered here and there are violas. Each flower combines yellow, white, and blue, its colors shared with its neighbors.

Wouldn't it be wonderful if human beings lived in such harmony? We could appreciate that we have much in common but that our differences make for interest and pleasure.

Deepak Chopra, MD[5] a prolific writer of international fame and respect, wrote in *The Book of Secrets* that we all are given the perfect model for living. He calls it the body's intelligence that occurs in our daily existence at the cellular level.

Each of the body's 250 different kinds of cells works for the well-being of the whole and will even die to protect it. Each cell is in continual communication with all the others and is flexible enough to adapt from moment to moment in response to immediate situations.

Cells recognize that they are all equally important. A liver cell is not more important than a skin or heart cell; they are interdependent. They know that they are fundamentally the same due to their genetic inheritance, and their primary task is maintaining the integrity of all other cells in the body. Although each type of cell has its unique functions, they can also combine in creative ways in response to novel stimuli. And every cell obeys the universal cycle of rest and activity, functioning on the smallest expenditure of energy possible, trusting that each will be provided all that it needs. They reproduce "in order to pass on their knowledge, experience, and talents, withholding nothing."

This is absolutely incredible!

Do you wonder why we ignore the perfect models given to us in nature and our own bodies? The truth is right before us, and we do not pay attention.

We fight wars (and always have) because we want everyone to be *just like us*, no matter who the "us" is with which we identify. We are certain that our beliefs are the right ones—the ones sanctioned by God. Have we forgotten that we all came from the same source? We act as if we are the ones who have the right to all the world's plenty.

There is no doubt that we are all on this finite world together. If we allow greed to be our master, we will all pay the price together.

Enjoy human diversity. It is not a threat; it is a blessing. There is room for it. It allows each of us to learn from as well as teach our neighbor.

Tolerance is a virtue. Acceptance is better yet.

Let's Talk

We communicate with our world all of the time, whether we acknowledge it or not, even when we isolate ourselves. (That in itself gives the message *I want time by myself.*) We communicate through our body posture, movement, facial expressions, and words. Verbal communication has its own nuances in volume, tone, and rate of delivery.

When I ask couples to identify what they perceive to be the biggest problem in their relationships, overwhelmingly, the answer given by both men and women is "communication." How is it that we don't know how to speak so that we feel heard? After all, most of us have been talking since we were toddlers!

There are a few rules that we are not necessarily taught that may help improve our communications with one another. They will take practice if they are not already your style and might feel awkward and artificial in the beginning. But keep in mind that there are few things we perform proficiently without practice—and sometimes we practice a skill in the wrong way for a long time!

You are the only one who knows what you are thinking or feeling until you share that thought or feeling with another. That makes you the authority on you! No one can tell you that you don't think or feel a particular way or that you *shouldn't* experience whatever you experience!

From that perspective, isn't it wise to talk from your authority? Begin by saying, "I think (or feel) …" and then state the thought or emotion and the cause of it. It might sound something like this: "I felt disappointed, because I was looking forward to seeing the movie with you as we planned, and then you didn't show up or call." Even as the offender, I can hardly argue with that. I may or may not offer explanation, but if I value our friendship, I will certainly apologize.

Let's use the same example with the complaint focused on the offender. It might be delivered in an angry or sullen manner and would sound closer to "You never keep your word. Once again, I waited and waited for you. I don't know why I bother. I should learn that you can't be trusted to follow through with anything." The experience was the same, but there is no identification or ownership of feelings, and it is stated as criticism and blame.

When we accuse and blame, especially if our accusations are accompanied by absolutes (*always* and *never,* for example), the offender is immediately on the defensive. It's human nature; if we feel attacked, we defend, even if we are in the wrong. Furthermore, the observed problem is now an attack on character and may very well escalate into more hurt feelings that could even threaten the friendship.

How often do you start with a desire to simply share an experience you had with another but sense that the other misunderstands you? Maybe they offer unsolicited advice on how you should respond to the situation or indicate that you are overreacting. Before you know it, you're in a shouting match, perhaps escalating into name-calling, and then you are off to the races. Words are said that were not intended; hurt is inflicted. This exchange becomes full of contempt (which is defined as a powerful feeling of dislike toward somebody or something considered to be worthless, inferior, or undeserving of respect).

Contempt is never allowed in communication. Commit yourself to staying in control. Yelling and name-calling are unproductive and always hurtful. Children who hear adults yelling at one another (and parents who yell at them) quickly lose respect. Take a time-out to gain composure, if need be, and come back to the discussion when you are more clear-headed and calm.

There is one more habit that is terribly harmful to good communication—stonewalling. The name fits the behavior perfectly, for the person who experiences it feels as if he or she is talking to a stone wall. These days, you might experience someone holding up his or her hand, implying that you "talk to the hand."

In essence, what you are saying to the other is, "I find you so undeserving of my time and attention, I will not even listen to you." This behavior has been around for a long time. I recently watched an old sitcom in which the husband hides behind his newspaper while his wife talks on and on. Occasionally, he mutters an "uh-huh," but he clearly is not engaged in what his wife is saying.

Don't engage in stonewalling. It is disrespectful and dismissive. If you find yourself distracted or unable to give the other your attention at that moment, claim it. "I'm sorry, but I just can't give you my full attention right now. I've had a hard day at work and need to clear my head. I am interested in what you have to say, so can it wait for thirty minutes or so?"

Following these guidelines will go a long way in improving the chance that your message is heard.

I've addressed only one half of the communication exchange. The other is the responsibility of the listener. I often wish we had classes like "Listening 101," but I have yet to find one. Giving our undivided attention to another is quite challenging; it is hard for us to silence our own reactions and responses long enough to hear another's message.

If we listen with our hearts and not just our ears, we create a win-win situation for both parties. That is the message of The Purple Hat.

The Purple Hat

This story is truly the finest example of abandoning oneself to love that I know. It speaks of stepping into the heart of the other and responding with empathy and understanding.

A remarkable woman became an admired friend after we shared the intimacy of massage. Good massage is truly intimate as two people share at a naked level (in more ways than one!) that is vulnerable and healing. In conversation after a session, she told me that she was really struggling with something that was important and had the potential to be life-changing for her.

This woman's love was a successful international corporate leader and is a very talented, dynamic man. He is artistic and creative, and many examples of his art are displayed in the beautiful, book-filled home they built when their sons were young. He is as accomplished in the kitchen as in the woodshop and can easily prepare a gourmet meal for a dozen friends that leaves the recipients feeling pampered and entertained. He was involved in many community charities and events and is a successful fundraiser and recruiter of others' talent. He is tall, handsome, gregarious, and fun!

The couple has three sons. All are now well-educated, bright, successful men. When they were finally independent, the time came for my friend to fulfill her own dreams, which were on hold during the busy years of family life. She enrolled in graduate school, completed her doctoral degree in children's literature, and was looking forward to writing books and perhaps doing a little teaching. She is also very talented and has a real flair for decorating and style. She is engaged in life but is more relaxed, quiet, and private than her husband. She is a beautiful woman and is full of creativity and fun. She used to say that her husband was the initiator and she was the appreciator. As I got to know her, I felt she was sometimes overwhelmed as the only woman in a house of men.

All in all, my friend and her husband created a wonderful, gracious life together. So what was the problem?

With the demands of school behind her, she looked forward to three years of more solitary days before her husband's planned retirement—days when she could move at her own pace, write her books, and enjoy company when *she* invited friends in. She would not have as many projects, places to be, or deadlines to meet. Her time would be quiet.

Then her husband came home from work one day and announced that he had submitted the paperwork for early retirement. After all, there were a million things he still wanted to do, and he needed the time to do them. She felt trapped. She loved her husband dearly and felt selfish for wanting so much just for herself—but she did want it. She didn't know how to tell him, because she didn't want to hurt his feelings, burst his bubble, or lead him to think she didn't enjoy his company. She was afraid that if she didn't say anything, she would become resentful.

We talked. And in answer to her question, "What am I going to do?" I replied, "You have to tell him." Later that week, as gently as she could, she did.

When next we met, she related that her husband listened, and after a bit, he said he understood; he knew he could be a bit over the top in his enthusiasm and involvement. Because he listened with his heart as well as his ears, he could see how hard it was for her to tell him what she needed and the conflict she felt when he talked about his plans for things to do.

But maybe if she didn't have to actually tell him every time she needed space, it would be easier for her. He knew she felt selfish and rejecting when saying the words, "I want to be alone." Instead, he told her that she could just put on her purple hat. That would be his signal that she needed some solitude, and he could give her that time without taking it personally or feeling wounded. He would give her space.

What an incredible gift! My friend's husband listened to her without filtering through the self or immediately responding with his own needs. He tried hard to understand her heart and the message intended. He truly did understand. It wasn't about him but about her. He knew that her love of self in no way diminished her love for him, and he could support and honor that.

My friend's relationship with her husband deepened with that response. He retired, and they moved to another city and bought a winter home in a warmer climate. She writes children's books, and he still gets involved in everything! Sometimes she joins him. They enjoy their children and grandchildren. They have a wonderful relationship that honors their time together ... and their time apart.

This is a love story.

Surprising Things Happen When We Listen

I experienced a lesson in listening at a Native American women's retreat. The task seemed impossible, but the results were astonishing.

The women in attendance were randomly divided into four groups of about a dozen. Each group was assigned one of the elements: fire, water, air, or earth. Our task was to create an original presentation that reflected the element assigned. It could be a story, poem, play, or dance—anything the entire presenting group agreed upon. We had a minimal amount of material—crepe paper, feathers, fabric, etc.—to create costumes or props. Incidentally, we had one hour before we would be called upon to present!

Have you ever been assigned to a committee at work with the objective of developing an operating procedure for a seemingly insignificant duty but had to meet week after week before a decision was finally made? Have you had one child refuse to budge from his room and whine that he wanted to go to the zoo when the rest of the family chose to go biking? Have you ever been assigned a group project at school only to find that each person had his or her own idea of how the task should be approached, and then the one or two most vocal members took over, and their ideas dominated? If you can identify with any of these scenarios, then you have been involved in group work.

After we gathered into our individual groups, a facilitator gave assignments (my group was given air) and handed the oldest member of each group a beautifully embellished stick that was about four feet long and perhaps two inches in diameter. This was the talking stick, and it was very powerful, because one was allowed to speak only when in possession of this stick. In our group, the oldest woman was a beautiful, wizened soul in her eighties who was an elder in her home community. She determined who would speak and for how long, for once she retrieved the stick, one's time was up. You could not ask for the stick and did not have any way of knowing when (or if) it would be your turn.

The first thing our elder suggested was that we close our eyes and think for the next five minutes about air and what that word conjured up inside of us. (Part of my time was spent thinking, *The clock is ticking! We were only given an hour!*) Then she handed the stick to the woman directly across from her, and that woman said she thought of air as life-giving and calm. A minute or two later, our elder retrieved the stick, and after a brief pause, she handed it to the woman seated to her right. This woman stated that she thought of air as powerful, with the capability of destroying. Again, a couple of minutes later, the elder retrieved the stick. It continued this way until every woman had voiced her thoughts about air.

There were no interruptions, and no one dominated the discussion. It was as if the process itself quieted the inner voice that was eager to be heard and allowed full attention to be given to what was said by another. (After all, there wasn't much else you could do!) Each contribution sparked recognition in me. "Yes! I know air that way, too!"

We presented a powerful enactment of air. There were a couple of women in repose, eyes closed, and smiles softening their features. Soft blue crepe paper streamers wrapped about their shoulders. They represented the life-giving, calm component. Other women strolled through the assembled group, trailing pastel-colored streamers and softly humming, gently stroking the cheeks and hair of the audience with feathers. They represented soft, cooling breezes. Some women stormed into the crowd, swirling black streamers through the assemblage, mussing hair, tipping over purses, and scattering papers about. They were air aroused to destructive force! In the end, we all joined the women in repose, indicating that air is always life-giving and that storms pass.

We were proud of the reception our presentation received. I was amazed that every woman's thoughts were incorporated into our dance. We had plenty of time, for when each was allowed to give voice to her thoughts without interruption or need to defend or persuade, we didn't get bogged down in the minutiae that often occurs in committees or groups.

Remarkable things can occur when we respectfully listen to our neighbor—even in an hour.

The Written Word

If I told you that I know of one of the most precious gifts that can ever be given, would I pique your curiosity? If I also told you that this gift can soothe the hurt of conflict as well as intensify the ecstasy of love, would you want to know more? If I shared that this gift was, in times past, given with regularity but is given only infrequently now and is as valuable to the giver as the receiver, could you guess what it is?

This gift is the written word—but not just any written word. It is the one that comes from your own hand.

Recall the little excitement of receiving a greeting card in the mail. Do you, like me, read the front of the card and appreciate the picture or decoration, but upon opening it, look immediately for what is handwritten? Have you ever been just a little disappointed when there is nothing but a signature, even if "Love" precedes it? The real joy comes from the thoughts of the sender, and they are greatly magnified by a handwritten line or two.

When I lived across the country from both my sons and was asked what I wanted one Mother's Day, I replied, "A letter." I could think of nothing that would please me more than what they shared of their busy lives, written in their own hand. Unlike flowers that would soon die or candy that my waistline would certainly never need, I savored their letters again and again. I smiled at the competition the letter writing became; each wanted his letter to be the first delivered, the longest, or the most creative. That was a great Mother's Day for me, even if I was far away from my sons. I still cherish those letters.

In a recent study of 193 soldiers who recently returned from combat, those who had received delayed but tangible letters had fewer symptoms of post-traumatic stress disorder (PTSD) than those who communicated via instant message and video chat. "These days, letters are relatively rare, so writing and sending one is a sign of commitment," says Howard Markham, PhD,[6] one of the University of Denver researchers in *The Journal of Traumatic Stress*.

The act of writing requires that we slow our thought processes so our hand can keep pace. (I often write letters in calligraphy to slow my thoughts even further.) Writing our thoughts out by hand provides the opportunity to edit before the thought is committed to paper. We can search for exactly the right word to express what we want the other to "hear." Our electronic devices forego all that. Fingers (and now thumbs) fly across keyboards, hit the send button, and it's done. (Sometimes, there really is finality because once sent, it is impossible to get back.)

Love letters come in many forms. They are expressions of devotion, admiration, and love as well as reminders of dreams and goals.

Committed to paper, they can be discovered over months and years amongst our treasures, tucked away, perhaps tied in ribbon.

In my experience, they never fail to bring the same warm feelings, even if the relationship has passed. Sometimes, like in the chapter on forgiveness, rereading a letter can be truly life-changing.

There is even more value to be discovered in the act of writing. Research suggests that when writing in response to hurt or anger, the act of writing itself eases the pain, and that can be enough; the letter doesn't even need to be sent. (Baike & Wilhelm, 2012: p. 338; Smyth & Pennebaker, 1999; p. 70). While words spoken in anger may know no gain or loss and often escalate a conflict, writing can have the opposite effect, dissipating the intensity of feeling and allowing for more clear-headedness when the opportunity for discussion actually arrives.

I often counsel couples to write one another when they have difficulty discussing an emotionally-charged subject that ended in argument or stalemate in the past. Once the emotional self takes center stage, it can be difficult to allow space for the other's perspective. We can't take back the words we've spoken in haste; letter-writing, on the other hand, almost invites self-reflection, as the thinking self takes over. It is not unusual to cross out a line or search for just the right word in an effort to convey a message or complaint in a less defensive, hurtful way. It may also be easier for the listener to "hear" the message delivered this way, because there is no immediate response required or even possible.

I believe humans need time to reflect, think past the instantaneous response that comes from the emotional, ego-centered self, and settle our minds before we react with words. When we take the time to write, we give the gift of time but also of timing. Often in communication, if the time is right for the speaker, there is little thought about whether the time is also right for the listener. For most of us, leaving an e-mail unopened or ignoring the little *ping* that notifies us we have a text message requires restraint we seldom have. For me, a letter is more like a little gift that waits for me to find a quiet moment to open, connect hearts as I conjure up the sender, and read and reread at my own pace, in my own time. It becomes a treasure.

A cherished friend told me about staying in touch with her dear, longtime friend who is in the beginning stages of Alzheimer's. At first, she called regularly, but she could tell that her friend tired and became confused even during short conversations. My friend started writing to her, sending her cards with brief, hand-written messages inside. Her friend was thankful and receptive and called when *she* felt up to conversation. More than that, she kept these little gifts handy to reread and appreciate. Despite her disability, she still had tangible evidence of the love of a friend.

Many cards and letters have been sent to me over the years. They are precious. I hope letter-writing becomes a habit for you. Don't always rely on Hallmark to pen the message. My experience tells me that *you* actually say it best.

Gifting

F amily members have been my dearest friends, mentors, and role models and have taught me what it means to gift someone.

Gifting in this context means participating in another's life whenever the opportunity arises. This was a lesson that Mother taught in my early childhood when she encouraged her children to join in wherever we found a need and do without being asked. There are many instances of this in my life. My sister helped me plan, organize, and prepare my first company dinner party, even though we were hundreds of miles apart. She called me every day to make sure I was on schedule so that the day my guests arrived, I appeared to be cool, calm, and collected.

Another sister devoted weeks to keeping contractors on schedule, painting and decorating my house while I worked halfway around the world. She unpacked boxes and organized my cupboards and closets, because she couldn't bear the thought of me returning to the mess I had left. My brother found and rebuilt a car for me—not once, but twice, after I blew up the engine—because I needed a car, and he wanted me to have a fun little sports car. My sister and brother-in-law came for a visit and spent much of their time doing countless little chores and fixing things around the house that I didn't know how to do myself. There are really too many instances for me to recount, but you get the message. I hope you can recall times when family or friends blessed you in similar ways.

I have often said, "How can I say 'I love you' if I have something in abundance that you need and I refuse to share it with you?" Well, that something is not limited to material things.

What is most important is that we participate in whatever happens in the moment. It doesn't really matter if you feel competent; just join in. Life isn't about being taken care of but rather about contributing in whatever way you can.

We all have been blessed; each of us has something to give. Gifts might come in little boxes with bows and ribbons, but gifts of time, skills, or whatever we have that will make another's day brighter are just as meaningful. It doesn't have to be perfect; maybe we're learning in the process, and that in itself can be treasured. Let the other know that you're thinking of and support him or her. Share the burdens as well as the fun. Remember, love is about what we give, not what we receive. When gifting is reciprocal, it's a beautiful dance of love!

Receiving Gifts

The way in which gifts are received is every bit as important as the way in which they are given.

Never take for granted what another person gives. Don't forget to be appreciative—ever. Don't demand. Don't try to manipulate, control, or assume that you have a right to what you were given. I use a lot of absolutes (always risky), but in this case, I mean them.

I'm intrigued by the way some people seem to change once they feel comfortable in a relationship. I've witnessed it more times than I would like to acknowledge. I advocate growth, but that's not the kind of change I am referring to. I'm talking about everything from forgetting good manners to being less than respectful, appreciative, and grateful.

Don't forget to be a best friend. If you wouldn't think of forgetting to thank acquaintances, casual friends, or strangers and be grateful for the kindnesses they show you without expectation of more to follow, then don't treat those closest to you with any less. It's important. Please be mindful in this area.

The Magic Number

Drs. John and Julie Gottman[7] have spent their careers carefully observing and analyzing married couples at the University of Washington and later at the Gottman Institute (The Love Lab). Their research has, in fact, enabled them to predict with more than 90 percent accuracy whether a married couple will stay together or eventually divorce. Statistically, that's pretty phenomenal.

Although predicting trouble is not the same as preventing it, I think what they have learned can help all of us become better at prevention. One finding that will improve the health of any relationship, if practiced regularly, could be world-changing. They call it the Magic Number.

It appears that those in happy, stable relationships make five positive remarks for every one negative remark, even when discussing conflict. They say you can think about this five-to-one ratio as akin to the pH of soil—the balance between acidity and alkalinity that is crucial to fertility. Relationships need much more positivity than negativity for nourishment. Without this balance, a relationship is in danger of withering and dying, just like a fragile vine that is planted in soil that is too acidic, sandy, or dry.

The Gottmans were working with couples, but I believe we could generalize this research with regard to everyone we encounter, for we are truly in relationships with everyone we meet, if only for a brief moment.

While working in Okinawa, I was gifted by a teacher and master calligrapher with a beautiful piece of his work. Translated from the ideograms, it literally means "one lifetime, one meeting." This suggests that each encounter, however brief, is an opportunity for an experience that will never occur again and hence should be cherished. It further suggests that in extending hospitality, one should endeavor to make each moment a memorable experience.

Isn't this a beautiful way to approach one another? I learned this lesson more personally in early adulthood.

During my father's long illness, one of his brothers, John, was faithful in making the three-hour trip to our home every week to visit with him. I didn't know Uncle Johnnie well and was, in fact, a bit intimidated by him during the few encounters I had with him as a child. Over the weeks, however, as I got to know him better, a very loving relationship developed between us.

After my father's death, I mentioned to my mother how important Johnnie became to me as I watched the love exchanged between brothers and witnessed him supporting her and me through the long days of caring and letting go. She said, "Jo, I'm really glad to hear that. But don't just tell me; tell him!"

That was good advice, because in doing so, I invited Johnnie to continue being a part of my life. He became an important familial figure; my life was enriched by his presence.

You can see that the opportunity to work for that five-to-one Magic Number presents itself frequently with both loved ones and strangers. We just have to be aware and make the extra effort to share it. It takes just a moment to give a sincere compliment that will most likely brighten another's day.

If this is not a habit for you now, begin. Keep an honest, daily, private account of how you're doing in meeting that magic number with loved ones, neighbors, and strangers. Eventually, it will become a habit—even when you're tired, out of sorts, or too busy. Do it for yourself. Over time, you may discover a change in your own outlook as you offer warm, positive regard to others.

Stress and the Family

Every generation experiences stress: economic hardship, unemployment, war, political strife. Grandparents lived through the Great Depression and World War II before life evened out in the fifties, and there seemed to be more stability. My generation started out in those good times (albeit with the overshadowing of the Cold War) and now has to face uncertainty as savings for retirement have been lost, unemployment and rising costs are again on everyone's mind, and our young folks are taken to fight the numerous wars on terrorism. The current generation is in the midst of all this, compounded by the sensationalistic media that adds to it every time you turn on the television or read a newspaper. We are bombarded with news of school violence, natural disasters, and globalization that threatens to take jobs away.

Stress helped our ancestors outrun the tiger; the nervous system immediately began firing, causing hormones to surge throughout the body to give that extra burst of energy and mobilize to meet the body's immediate needs. When the danger passed (either because the tiger was outrun or the tiger enjoyed a meal!), stress ended, and those physiological responses returned to normal levels. Without that stress reaction, we probably wouldn't be around to discuss this.

While stress can be a problem, it is too simplistic to see it only in a negative light. Stress was actually designed to be a lifesaver. An appropriate level of stress helps us perform well in our jobs and energizes students to practice for recitals or train for races. Without it, we could become lethargic. Problems arise, however, when stress becomes chronic or we don't manage our stress level well.

The twenty-first-century crises that I've listed, to name just a few, require intense efforts for survival. But most of the events that cause stress are not life-threatening—a fight with a spouse, pressure at work, financial worries, and the ongoing challenge of balancing the demands made on our time and resources will not cause our demise. Yet our bodies are not designed to meet those stressors day after day. It would be good if physically, we responded appropriately to the different levels of stress, but we only have the hormones that prepare us to escape from the tiger.

Stress can be a significant contributor to ill health. Generally, this is because people who are stressed are more likely to do whatever it takes to find relief; they smoke, eat too much, spend too many hours engaged in virtual entertainment, or use alcohol or drugs. Emotions also play an important role in how we experience stress and what we choose to do about it.

Find good coping mechanisms that will enhance your health and happiness instead of replacing one problem with yet another. Make your choices good examples for your children. Use your influence wisely.

Competence,
Confidence, and Pride

While working in Okinawa, Japan, I stayed on the seventh
floor of the ocean-side Kafuu Resort Fuchaku. The view
of the artfully planned pathways wending through the gently
sloping, beautifully manicured, flower-laden foliage to the white
sand beach and the China Sea was breathtaking. By day, the
continually changing cloud formations over this small island were
entrancing, and at night, without much ambient light from below,
the sky was peppered with more stars than I had ever seen.

I spent many of my early morning and evening hours
delighting in the panorama of the ocean, sky, and lights of
travelers moving along a coastal highway from one nearby town
to another. As utopian as this might sound, it is also true that
Okinawa in July and August is steaming, with temperatures in
the hundred-degree range and humidity levels to match. During
the relatively cooler temperatures of night, the moisture in the air
condensed on every glass surface, obscuring this beautiful scene
with dripping water.

From my balcony, I could also look down on the swimming pool area; to my left was the adjacent parking lot. One early Saturday morning, I was enjoying my coffee on the balcony while the temperatures were still cool enough to be inviting and noticed a hotel crew of six at work. They all appeared to be in their teens or slightly older, and I enjoyed their banter and the occasional laughter that drifted up to me. After diligently tidying the pool area, they moved on to the parking lot.

I was curious about what they would find to do there, as I could see no litter to be picked up or plantings to trim—only a lot of fifty or so parked cars. As I watched, they began to wipe the condensation from every window, headlight, and mirror of the vehicles parked closest to the hotel entrance. My first thought was that this was a service for the VIP guests so their cars would be ready for them without the nuisance of having to dry the windows themselves. How nice.

The work crew attended to their task with great care. These young workers used cloths that needed to be wrung out after each vehicle was dried—not nearly as efficient as a squeegee, although probably producing a more thorough result. I soon realized that this service was not just for the very important guests, as I had assumed, but included all the vehicles in the lot, for my rental car received the same attention as those preceding it. As I watched, one of the workers turned to scrutinize his completed work and returned to touch up what he must have considered a less than adequate job.

There were no car owners waiting to offer a tip and no supervisor to critique their work or keep them on task. Rather, they did an assigned job and undertook the task with efficiency and good spirit. I witnessed what pride-in-the-making might look like—how even a menial task might contribute to the development of a healthy value placed on personal efforts and achievements and the proper sense of one's own worth.

I began thinking about how self-esteem develops. Self-esteem doesn't really come from the praise of others, although we might enjoy that affirmation. Our internal voices are the true barometers of whether or not we performed well, were critical enough to address areas where improvement was needed, and were tenacious enough to persist until satisfied that expected high standards were met. When we engage in a task in that spirit, we gain competence—the knowledge that we are capable of proficiency—and from that, confidence is born. Confidence then becomes part of our internal dialogue, so when faced with a novel task, there is already evidence that we can perform well if we don't give up until we attain mastery. Only through our own efforts do we earn justifiable pride—self-esteem's staunchest companion.

As a counselor, I have often heard the self-identified complaint of low self-esteem. Personally, I was blessed with parents who encouraged curiosity and adventure, praised effort rather than results as a new skill was practiced, and did not see imperfection as failure or a source of shame. My siblings and I grew up in a time that allowed more freedom and security; parental teachings were reinforced by four older siblings who constantly reminded me that if I couldn't keep up, I would have to go home. I learned to challenge myself until my abilities were more in line with my determination.

If you didn't enjoy that kind of childhood or self-doubt and insecurity resulted from unfortunate life experiences, there is still an avenue to improved self-esteem and confidence that has perhaps been overlooked. Listen to the voice that admires a work of art or music, or notice when a garden or landscape catches your eye, and then create the opportunity to explore your own creativity in that area. Perhaps you have talents as an artist, musician, photographer, or gardener that lie dormant, waiting for expression. In the beginning, you will need those same ingredients taught by my parents:

- curiosity and a desire to learn
- praise for effort rather than results
- persistence
- reasonable expectations

Although these principals can be applied to most any undertaking, developing a hobby is one readily available to everyone. If you don't currently have a hobby, find one. You may have a few false starts until you discover the pastime that truly ignites your passion, but it's worth the exploration. As you hone your skills, it is likely that you will develop a more critical eye, evaluation and expectations will change, and you may seek out classes or experts who can help you past what is self-taught. Eventually, you will experience the pride that comes when someone compliments you on the sweater you're wearing (that, of course, you knit yourself), someone asks for a copy of the nature pictures you shared around the office (that you took using your newly acquired camera lens), or you are asked for the recipe of a dessert that you created. The possibilities are endless.

There are secondary rewards to these activities that will also increase self-esteem. You might develop new relationships with people who share your interests. You will become a participant rather than a bystander. Participation offers challenges and opportunities for growth, satisfaction, and great pleasure as you move toward proficiency. We cannot expect those results if we live vicariously.

Final Thoughts

What I have written comes from my own life experiences. I wish I could tell you that I have mastered all that I have presented here, but I cannot. I continue to struggle as I try to remember what is important. Sometimes I'm on my A-Game, but often I come up short. I continue to be enmeshed in life, just like you, but I strive to be more mindfully aware.

There are values I know to be imperative to healthy living. One I have repeated throughout this book is the value of responsibility. I have made a lot of mistakes, but I strive to take responsibility for my actions. I can be impatient, grouchy, and less of a friend than I would like to see myself. But when I take a moment to think about my actions or inactions, I find that most of the time, I am the only one at fault.

Life is a gift from nature that we enjoy for just a brief period of time. Some of us get to hang around longer than others, but we all pass. Your life holds much promise for you. How you live it is your choice.

My hope is that as you read through this book, you become mindful of your own life's lessons, teachers, and experiences. These written words are useful reminders for me and might serve to give food for thought to my children, grandchildren, and you.

Much of what I have written seems beautifully summarized in a poem penned by Max Ehrmann (c. 1920) that I discovered many years ago. Its name is Latin and translates to "desired things." May you also find beauty in its message.

The Desiderata

G o placidly amid the noise and haste, and remember what peace there may be in silence.

As far as possible, without surrender, be on good terms with all persons. Speak your truth quietly and clearly, and listen to others—even to the dull and the ignorant—they, too, have their story. Avoid loud and aggressive persons; they are vexations to the spirit.

If you compare yourself with others, you may become vain and bitter, for always there will be greater and lesser persons than yourself. Enjoy your achievements as well as your plans. Keep interested in your own career, however humble; it is a real possession in the changing fortunes of time.

Exercise caution in your business affairs, for the world is full of trickery. But let this not blind you to what virtue there is; many persons strive for high ideals, and everywhere, life is full of heroism. Be yourself. Especially, do not feign affection. Neither be cynical about love, for in the face of all aridity and disenchantment, it is perennial as the grass.

Take kindly to the counsel of the years, gracefully surrendering the things of youth. Nurture strength of spirit to shield you in sudden misfortune. But do not distress yourself with imaginings. Many fears are born of fatigue and loneliness.

Beyond a wholesome discipline, be gentle with yourself. You are a child of the universe, no less than the trees and the stars; you have a right to be here. And whether or not it is clear to you, no doubt the universe is unfolding as it should.

Therefore be at peace with God, whatever you conceive Him to be, and whatever your labors and aspirations, in the noisy confusion of life, keep peace in your soul.

With all its sham, drudgery, and broken dreams, it is still a beautiful world.

Be cheerful. Strive to be happy.

The Continuation
of Your Love Story

I have purposely left these pages blank for you to record your own experiences and thoughts as you continue on your life journey. I hope you choose to use them.

Bibliography

Arnold, Jeanne E., et al. *Life at Home in the Twenty-first Century: 32 Families Open Their Doors*. Hong Kong: The Cotsen Institute of Archeology Press, 2012.

Baikie, K. & Wilhelm, K. (2012). Emotional and physical health benefits of expressive writing. In *Advances in Psychiatric Treatment*. (ed. P. Casey). pp. 338-346. London: The Royal College of Psychiatrists.

Center for Disease Control. *Morbidity and Mortality Weekly Report/* September 2, 2011/Vol. 60 (Suppl): Mental Illness Surveillance Among Adults in the United States.

Chopra, Deepak, MD. *The Book of Secrets*. New York: Three Rivers Press, 2004.

Gottman, John M., PhD and Gottman, Julie S., PhD. *10 Lessons to Transform Your Marriage*. New York: Three Rivers Press, 2007.

Howe, Marie. *What the Living Do*. New York: W. W. Norton and Company, Inc., 1998.

Kabat-Zinn, Jon, PhD. *Wherever You Go, There You Are*. New York: Harper Collins Publishing, 2004.

Markham, H., PhD et al, (in press). "Relationships between Soldiers' PTSD Symptoms and Spousal Communication During Deployment," in the *Journal of Traumatic Stress*.

Smyth, J.M. & Pennebaker, J.W. (1999) Sharing one's story: translating emotional experiences into words as a coping tool. In *Coping: The Psychology of What Works*. (ed. C. R. Snyder), pp. 70-89. New York: Oxford University Press.

Made in the USA
Middletown, DE
24 September 2021